PIERROT

ACKNOWLEDGEMENTS

Some of these poems have been published in *Agenda*; *Almost Island*; *ArtsEtc*; *Bim*; *The Caribbean Writer*; *Connotation Press: An Online Artifact*; *The Ekphrastic Review*; *Humber Literary Review*; I*nterviewing the Caribbean*; *The Missing Slate*; *Punch* (India); *The Puritan*; *Re-Markings*; *Temenos Academy Review* 22; *Visual Arts Magazine Barbados*; and in *City Remembrances: poems* (2016); *Song & Symphony* (2016).

Many of these poems were inspired by the art of artists who are named.

For brief quotations from the work of Dionne Brand, Vahni Capildeo, Aimé Césaire, Leonard Cohen, Hart Crane, Hilary Davies, Kwame Dawes, John Donne, David Hinds, Billie Holiday, Li-Young Lee, Robert Lowell, Canisia Lubrin, Bob Marley, Friedrich Nietzsche, Philippe Petit, Psalms, Steel Pulse, Francis Thompson, Derek Walcott, William Wordsworth.

Cover art by Shallon Fadlien – *at the heart of the mask*, 2015. Ms. Fadlien is a Saint Lucian artist resident in Oshawa, Ontario, Canada. Author photo: Veronica Lee

Author's note: The inspiration for the Pierrot figure came from the cover painting by Shallon Fadlien. The eyes and mouth reveal the person beneath the costume, the actor under the masquerade, with all his heart pain, bewilderment, anguish. This Pierrot is a composite of the Trinidad early carnival character Pierrot, the later Pierrot Grenade, verbose Midnight Robber, Saint Lucian New Year masqueraders, including Papa Djab. He is also a Christ figure, the Man of Sorrows.

JOHN ROBERT LEE

PIERROT

PEEPAL TREE

First published in Great Britain in 2020
Peepal Tree Press Ltd
17 King's Avenue
Leeds LS6 1QS
UK

© John Robert Lee 2020

All rights reserved
No part of this publication may be
reproduced or transmitted in any form
without permission

ISBN 13: 9781845234782

CONTENTS

PART ONE

Pigeon Island	9
Sketches and Canticles of Lent	10
Letter: after Dionne Brand	12
Lepidoptera: after Lorette, artist	14
Song & Symphony: after Shallon Fadlien	15
After Francis Thompson	20
Hyphen	23
Archetypes: after Jallim Eudovic	25
White Cedar	26
Sint Maarten	28
Rites: after Mosera	30
The Joseph Canticles	32
Mythos	34
After the Psalmist: a Song of Ascents	37
Doors: after Corrie Scott	39
Love Poem: after Mosera	41
One of us has Died	42
Haiku: at 70	44
Masquerade: for Garth St. Omer 1931-2018	45
Petroglyphs and Pictographs: after Ron Savory 1933-2019	47

PART TWO

1. Desperate notes	51
2. In the year that Shadow died	54
3. Mystery sentences Himself to dance in solitary	58
4. And then came those caped crusaders	62
5. Who made me a stranger in my world?	64
6. ars poetica	68
7. The photos in obituary pages still surprise us	71

for
Vladimir Lucien, Dionne Brand and the accomplished poets,
here and gone
Shallon Fadlien, Gary Butte, and the accomplished artists,
photographers, sculptors, here and gone
Jeremy Poynting and Hannah Bannister, Peepal Tree Press
Anne Walmsley

And for those who love me.

In Memoriam:
Rhona Pilgrim, Bookseller 1939 - 2019
Ron Savory, Artist, 1933 - 2019
Winston Bailey, The Mighty Shadow, 1941-2018

I am the Alpha and the Omega, the Beginning and the End, the First and the Last. — Jesus Christ (Revelation 22:13).

O my Sycamore Tree, saw the Freedom Tree — Bob Marley

... I
enter, without retreat or help from history,
the days of no day, my earth
of no earth, I re-enter

the city in which I love you.
And I never believed that the multitude
of dreams and many words were vain. — Li-Young Lee

PART ONE

PIGEON ISLAND
(for Raphael 'Rinvelle' Philip, artist)

> ...And I have felt
> A presence that disturbs me with the joy
> Of elevated thoughts; a sense sublime
> Of something far more deeply interfused...
> – Wordsworth "Lines Composed a Few Miles Above Tintern Abbey"

    Do angels congregate here, in this place?
Pigeon Island no more an island –
a pleasant park fringed by temperamental ocean

coming through dwarf palms,
combing surf cresting under wind-heavy casuarinas
and small boats busy off the balcony

of Jambe de Bois café. Mixed multitudes
clamber through the old fort and ruins
of the officers' mess, braving the precipitous path

to the sphinx-head peak; undulating
lawns host seasons of tumbling children,
jazz aficionados, an occasional theatre troupe.

    Me, I love the ascending leaf-strewn way to the curving spine
that leads to musing about angels,
arriving again at a certain flower-charged cedar that looks out
    over the bay,

then coming down, to sit gazing
at promiscuous surf collapsing forever
all over the wet, unyielding stones.

SKETCHES AND CANTICLES OF LENT
— *after Shallon Fadlien, artist*

i. *Pierrot — Mardi Gras*

Filthy feathers, that painted shoe, trampled headpiece, etcetera,
choking drains down the route;
street-light blinking out; stale roti

baddening the guts, your eyes sharp for midnight bandit
or coke jumbie looking to make ole-mas
with the unwary.
                      You, clown prince, you celebratory idiot,

you forget she was Coolie Devil original,
Jab-Jab Mistress, maker of scourges?

ii. *Socialite — Ash Wednesday*

God, to be outta this talk-show bakanal,
these infernal cycles of mamaguy kaiso politricks,
perpetual, shameless, cell-phone scandals
and all else — man gone cold in Toronto,
landlord looking for his portion,
me sleeping with my fantasies;

            in the penitential procession
the priest and his boys washing
you, beloved masquerader, in their platter of ashes.

iii. *Masque – Good Friday*

We know the triumphant end of that old scenario:
disembowelled shroud, vacant catacomb,
incredible gossip of love-struck women

whose eyes and hands and arms
encompassed the impossible incarnate eternal,
the risen God.
                       The empty mask, inanimate

signature of death's humanity
crosses to centre-stage before that tremendous denouement.

LETTER
after Dionne Brand: a glosa variation

all I can offer you now though is my brooding hand,
my sodden eyelashes and the like,
these humble and particular things I know,
my eyes pinned to your face. — Dionne Brand (Inventory)

                        I must tell you how moved I was,
          astonished perhaps, like the wind's castanets in palms
               outside my window, like the chak-chak of shells

under the interfering proddings of surf —
how you drew me close, yes, to brimming
over your so-unexpected full-veined

lines that were the archetypal echo
humming under my breath
and, indeed, here you were, Brand,

— all I can offer you now though is my brooding hand —

                      parsing your notations, perusing your inventory
                            of our blasted days, Aleppo now
                        and then Nice and yesterday Orlando

tomorrow Laventille again, Trench Town recurrent
Richmond Hill impossible to forget —
ossuaries, yes, of failed states and their politricks

babies broken on beaches, Mediterranean
drowned in overladen caravels
our islands' doomed alleys mocking

my sodden eyelashes and the like —

                  exhausting, these post-modern certainties
                        no truth, no meaning, no author,
           no beauty I suppose in the old songs of remembering

upon drum, string and bones
dimpled laugh of the old woman who loves you,
long arms of the dancer from San Fernando,

sacramental light rimming the ends of sunsets,
languid cruising of scissor-tailed seabirds
through our horizons, reading a fine poet from Toronto –

these humble and particular things I know,

                  add thresholds of jalousied doorways I crossed
              pursuing mystery love, drawn even then by the echo
                  quivering on metronomes of evening softnesses

to find faith waiting in lines of dread-locked canticles
pointing couplets of dark sayings
terrible chapters of mighty prophecies.

Anyway, like some minor April epiphany,
I'm downtown Port of Spain, corner Hart & Abercromby
and you reading, tenderly, at Bocas

my eyes pinned to your face

LEPIDOPTERA: AFTER LORETTE, ARTIST

>   Of course, each life matters
>   the embryonic and the homeless,
>   those lost to themselves in muttering

frenzies of precipitous days,
the rubble-shrouded children of Aleppo,
crucified saints of Sudan

coke-heads of Manila,
and the trans-gendered below Kingston's ghettos.
But these gone lives I particularly know:

young Trayvon, breath-stopped Eric, distraught
Sandra Bland, many who should be living now –
and somewhere, in a civilized, suburban basement,

this child also, among the lepidopterist's cases
collecting nightmares in the formaldehyde
of an old man's lusts,

>   pinned to this daguerreotype of a sketch,
>   she matters, she matters

SONG & SYMPHONY: AFTER SHALLON FADLIEN

> *And so it was I entered the broken world*
> *To trace the visionary company of love…*
> — Hart Crane

Overture: Rainbow in Balata

A story for you:
    In late afternoon drizzle,
coming home through familiar Balata
– its blossoming gardens of mangoes, gloricidia

and palms' branches like multi-winged cherubim – in that light
I saw a huge rainbow, close as heaven, spectrum a palette
of red to indigo with her sister violet,

    the end down a footpath
settled like a full-bodied beauty on a bench
under a breadfruit tree, there off Balata.

    This true story is for you and the un-looked-for embrace
in the arms of your tender-hued interest,
which surprised me, coming round this bend, like that *arc-en-ciel,*

1st Movement

  which surprised me, coming round this bend, like that *arc-en-ciel.*
    Oh, let us not leave too early the crotons and embracing coralita
          around the garden seat, the refracting light, not till

we have to, not till I've looked enough at you, separate
and particular, to find my fool of a fantasy,
my illiterate, ignorant, simpleton desire

flashing for a startling instant between us
like the last sunlight of the day
off the unruly bougainvillea

and the intrusive, beckoning band of your ring

                      and the intrusive, beckoning band of your ring
                          extent and boundary of my fancies –
                              stripped to the soul of things.

After the pouting bridesmaids, obligatory dances,
leering innuendos, begins the marrying of souls
in sacred ceremony, begins the long quest for entrances,

and when, at last, we note the viola's insistent echo
from whatever morne or valley, of the one lip
like the one name, that is ours to sing, we go

in, to the heart of the matter of, yes my love, love

                      in, to the heart of the matter of, yes my love, love
                          despite cynical academies, gossiping sidewalks
                              and wary pews, oh, let us not leave

too soon our fervent faces, our eyes plotting
new maps like amateur cartographers
clambering hand and foot over these rocks,

these protuberances of limiting biographies
these harbingers of coming failure.
Oh, let us not leave these arms, hollow and faithless

till we come beyond us, in sight of ourselves, waiting

                      till we come beyond us, in sight of ourselves, waiting
                          coupled, singular, familiar
                              in love, without ambiguous twilight.

Do not say, from the garden's crepuscular
shadows, between the last settling cedar blossoms,
'You are funny… didn't know you were mystical.'

You doubt the reason of love's awesome
revelations? You know the transfigured companion
at ease upon your breast? You think consummation

ends here, in the tossed sheets of your ego?

                        Ends here, in the tossed sheets of your ego,
               the first road, the simple path, the blessed erotic.
                              Can you take the *Purgatorio*

in black and blue of solitary guitars
desperate, hoarse trombones
and, over dangerous city alleys, wailing reggae?

Oh darling, let us hear now the spiralling symphonies
and songs, in keys major or minor,
of our earth's orchestrated premonitions

the chastening chords of dark passages, the discordant notes.

2nd Movement

      The chastening chords of dark passages, the discordant notes,
              the purging interludes of sorrow find their end.
        And after, here you are, with patient hand you've waited

for our days turned round and over, yesterday, tomorrow,
certain now. And I remember (do you?)
across the valley, the viola's echo

and that epiphanic evening of the garden rainbow
when we knew we were in love's unambiguous light.
Oh, don't say you have forgotten that promise of *Paradiso,*

the beatific heart of the matter of, yes my faithful love, love –

    the beatific heart of the matter of, yes my faithful love, love.
              In the mean time, the blessed ordinary:
        the broom-seller at the corner, karaoke bar above

the grocery, raisin bread and custards from Coral Street
for your tea, measuring medications,
nodding over the evening news, settling our backs into our corners.

Can this make a song, a certain melody
drawn from your old guitar, this companionship –
soft, aromatic as aging incense – these remembrances,

that persistent chord coming through the hibiscus hedge.

        That persistent chord coming through the hibiscus hedge
            like a Patrick St. Eloi tender mazouk:
              come, shake the legs free of this age,

its idolatry of death, crutches of belly-aching,
damned numbing noise without living rhythm,
paralysis of those who limp with crippling pride in the dark.

Come, a last close rubadub to bass and drum,
heart to heart, breast to lifting breast,
and oh, we've kept it all, we've kept the time.

Now, let us go in, leave the dark garden.

        Now, let us go in, leave the dark garden
      to the coralita, crotons and fragrance of spider-lilies
    guavas and golden-apples somewhere in their shadows.

Again I hear the distant orchestra's echo, strings and horns,
a solo cantor and, do you hear, our name in the song.
Come the threshold of night, we shall meet ourselves

in love, without ambiguous twilight, coupled, singular,
familiar, embraced in doorways of rainbow light,
separate and particular, and leave behind forever

the sliver-season of the moon

Finale: "the sliver-season of the moon"

The sliver-season of the moon
has come round again
over the hill-quarter of Monier –

from Grande Rivière the avenue
climbs through blossoming Lent:
    yellow avocado, golden-browning menorahs

    of mango, the exuberant
    lavender of glory-cedar;
below the roofs and branches
fluorescent Corinth and Marisule edge
the evening ocean.
                    Your love returns

certain as the lunar's phasing of its age,
as the pulsing of hearts and petals,
as the approaching bulk of hill

grows itself a dark wedge
against the sliver-season of the moon.

> *The difficult I'll do right now*
> *The impossible will take a little while.*
>   – Billie Holiday

AFTER FRANCIS THOMPSON (1859-1907):
A glosa variation

The angels keep their ancient places; —
Turn but a stone, and start a wing!
'Tis ye, 'tis your estrangèd faces,
That miss the many-splendoured thing.
— Francis Thompson (The Kingdom of God)

I.
The year ended in rubbled apartments and burnt mosques of Aleppo,
bloody alleys of Mosul, assaulted Christmas market of Berlin,
airliners' debris over Medellin and the Black Sea,
haunted by YouTube shadows of Cohen, Prince, Fidel…

Death masks in the mirror,
joins the ticker parade of funny faces

prancing in their jackboots under the towers of 5th Ave
while refugee tents ghetto the borders of Europe.

Be sure in any case
the angels keep their ancient places; —

II.
Here, titanic ships rise above our main-street banks;
passengers negotiate sidewalk vendors, hustling taxis,
repetitive tours, pray they won't be mugged. On Facebook,
pics of another hanging man, bloody pavements and viral texts.

Party-hacks dominate talk-shows, men posture in irrelevant parliaments
election bells are rung, and polls get it wrong

again. At end of year, accountants manipulate statements
of hurricane, earthquake and beach-front loss to expatriate profit.

When you pause near guava, lime and avocado gardens with a prayer
	and a song,
turn but a stone, and start a wing!

III.
You pass the commerce of tattooed intersections, the beauty-parlour
	business of Babylon,
engraved cynicisms pleating painted eyebrows, gossip of miseries
	broad-thighed in doorways
and iPhones' twitter from palms of selfie millennials turning
	corners of rumour
into traffic of fake news. December stumbles with sudden deaths
	of the famous

and the victim, past predictable headline griefs, to champagne
	boat-rides,
midnight fireworks, infidelities, intimations of apocalypse.
	Where, what, why are the plumbed depths of all that going
from bus-stand to cake-shop to Syrian store to passport office
	to morgue?

On the palimpsest of your defiant erasures
'tis ye, 'tis your estrangèd faces

become alien signature, distracted, tone-deaf
to your own primal keening,
under the craving to be touched, to be kneaded
	at the turning of the year.

IV.
In sight of 70, anticipating retreat,
I know the Kingdom's door will swing
to receive me soon some new year morning.

Beyond my fool of a heart that loves the slant-eyes of Egypt,

let me not be found among the self-deceiving
that miss the many-splendoured thing.

HYPHEN
for Austin 'Tom' Clarke 1934- 2016

To me, it's really so simple: life should be lived on the edge. You have to exercise rebellion, to refuse to tape yourself to the rules, to refuse your own success, to refuse to repeat yourself, to see every day, every year, every idea as a true challenge. Then you will live your life on the tightrope.
— Philippe Petit, tight-rope walker.

I.   high wire

                The figure in black called his dangerous act a 'coup';
the press: 'outrageous', 'audacious', 'artistic crime of the century'.
         I imagine the abyss of New York below his tight-rope.

Crazy man. The photos disturb
my gut. Angels had to have held him up.
Suppose he had fallen like a demon to the kerbs

of Lower Manhattan? Too high for me that science, stupefying
such aerial defiance on the inch-wide edge of the brink –
on the thin wing of his pole, sauntering that stratosphere

        indestructible. Ask: who scripted 9/11 and all that broke
          and fell into itself that day, those girders, those heights,
    the falling man, the conflagrated wires, the vaporised ropes?

II.   hyphen

                The black, dread-locked figure of Tom Clarke
                  crosses the cold, clear span of the hyphen
                      of Canadian space, striking
out over the white vast of its lakes, plains
diasporic cities and other chasms,
stepping between ziggurats of Babylon,

their steel and glass tablets of encrypted racism
negotiating the insistent subtraction of face from nation –

On the fiction of *his* pole, his arrogance striding those high places,

        he defies thin thresholds of fear, for Albert Johnson,
            Emmet Till, Soweto, the charred churches
        for Malcolm, Nina Simone, his chattel-house Bajans.

ARCHETYPES:
After Jallim Eudovic, sculptor

i.
The first lintel, threshold and jambs
the first frame on his space
the first stepping under beams
of dawning light in his house
      – first mirror, first tomb.

ii.
The first water-carrier
first beauty of soft breasts
first grace of hip and curving
neck, first insistent pleas
of the first son, the tiller.

iii.
First harvest under a haloed moon
after scattered seeds, first sweat-filled furrows –
the first wine with the first men
first innocent flirtations
      – then came the first goddesses under sheaves of corn.

iv.
The first embalming shroud swaddled the first shepherd,
our first love, and we lifted him
to the first sun of the first hour, every day for nine days of sacred
remembrance – then the holy mound
received his sarcophagus, on stretched skins of the first lamb and first
      leopard.

WHITE CEDAR

In memoriam Derek Walcott 1930-2017: a glosa variation

Make room for the accommodation of the dead,
their mounds that multiply by the furrowing sea,
not in the torch-lit catacombs of your head
but by the almond-bright, spume-blown cemetery.
              — Derek Walcott (*The Prodigal*)

I.

          I thought it was over, the season of lilac carpets
              along verges, on green lawns,
                 petals of *powyé* stepping off currents

of soft air, settling with tender ease on earth's lanes,
but here they are again, in May, everywhere,
with the mourning bassoon of wood doves, and yes indeed,

incredibly, to me ignorant of seasons of flora,
I see the fragrant Easter spider-lily
blooming from unexpected corners of my without-you days.

Make room for the accommodation of the dead,

                 you muttered, in a dark saying
                 that seemed to mute memory,
          to remove yourself to needle-leaved casuarinas

of Pigeon Island, out of our too familiar embrace,
too smothering adulation, our burrowing eyes
searching out your diaries.

II.
And the cascading cedar blossoms
race the grey heron to surf-chastened ledges of Becune Point
the forlorn pool, deserted studio, vacant easel, and

their mounds that multiply by the furrowing sea,

    after gentle curtsies through golden late afternoons
      to lakonmèt and Martiniquan mazouk,
    past delicate carvings of white-cedar figurines

in the sculptor's garden and other such benedictions.

III.
  Meantime, autocrats of Mammon desecrate your groves
    and beaches.
They set iron beasts to holy roots of the blessed cedar with
  arrogant pride,

they mock the memory of your protests;
they will not heed angry alarums of scissor-tailed gulls,
stubborn silence of drought, so we want your grey-eyed fierceness *here*

not in the torch-lit catacombs of your head

      not in tiresome fictions of some mythical you
      but impossibly, like Atlantic breakers
    glimpsed through bamboo off violated Praslin, *here, now.*

IV.
Heraldic egrets lift your lines
from Morne Fortune to Moule a Chique
with the awkward grace of their perfect symmetry,

the flowering mauve of cedar
tumbles through green fern around Soufriere
and we leaf your last book, not near your beloved bent Piton

but by the almond-bright, spume-blown cemetery.

SINT MAARTEN
(for —)

i.
The Blue Bitch Bar, on the boardwalk
behind Front Street, Philipsburg,
was where we read, Friday night,
during the Book Fair.
Dogs chased kids on Segways,
a band played Third World classics,
waitress gave me the wireless password,
patrons were polite,
writers applauded each other
    and you reminded me
    of someone I loved, and who loved me
    45 years ago.

ii.
"Casino country," said a friend,
and downtown, lining narrow, cobbled streets,
jewellery stores everywhere, with elderly women
who get a tip if you enter and buy;
a yellow antique car decorates Old Street,
Indian shops offer deals on saris and iPads,
and back at the book tables, you sign – faith
for a young one who believes
in more than cruise-ship terminals –
    but we can't go back, you and I
    to undivided lives, to love as simple
    as pelicans browsing uninvaded shallows.

iii.
At Boundary Monument, driving to Marigot
Shujah points out the flag of the movement
for a united St. Martin –
no more French lagoon, or Dutch salt pond
a mosaic "island of dreams", multi-national, multi-lingual

cosmopolitan Caribbean.
I didn't see enough
of bay-embraced quartiers and small hills
to measure the fantasy,
>	like bridging the points
>	between archived nostalgia
>	and relentless vague desire.

RITES: AFTER MOSERA, ARTIST

i.
No news to me, news of my death
though telebituaries trace coordinates
of relative history;

news-clips flatter their distortions
and those who loved me
research the corners

of archived regrets,
fictions of our passings,
to see the first passions

of hand-in-hand, intimate desires,
before we seduced ourselves
with silly distractions.

No news to me, news of my death
among the shades of Sheol.

ii.
In the end was the hating word
and that was that;
I knew the track to end the world

under the almonds,
cruising scissor-tails,
a beckoning horizon of pewter ocean,

but you came, a curious brown heron,
standing like a sea-stone on one foot,
fixed me to your insistent life

until I let the fool of a man
go drown.

iii.
It wasn't all needles and cracked hoes
in the far city, homeless under aqueducts
wrestling filthy strays over pizza boxes.

In the beginning, beautiful companions
jazz clubs, hit shows,
late-night coffee and smoke in penthouse studios;

names and faces of the day, Basquiat on the wall,
soap-opera romantics with heiresses –
the predictable, worthless fantasies.

Those who loved me I broke
under the guilt on my fatherless back.

iv.
Talitha, errant mythologies notwithstanding,
truth be told, Mystery calls through traffic
and sound-systems of Jeremie Street

on Friday evening, looks over the shoulder at you
on the pedestrian crossing;
is the unknown number ringing your phone

in a bank queue,
when you fall beyond dream
into alien, torrid shadows.

Mystery is the somehow familiar, tender wing
that lifts you to Himself.

THE JOSEPH CANTICLES

And Joseph made ready his chariot, and went up to meet Israel his father, to Goshen, and presented himself unto him; and he fell on his neck, and wept on his neck a good while...And Israel said unto Joseph, I had not thought to see thy face: – Genesis 46:29, 48:11.

i.
"It's the coat, multi-hued, seamless,
torn off my shoulder, and torn,
torn like the rent clothes

of Israel's inconsolable grief and mourning,
that arrays anxious dreams of court intrigue,
visions that recur of doors of no returning.

Enslavements hold fast their rings;
their vestures threaten sudden loss.

ii.
Another garment spoke another lie,
folded in the lonely arms
of that full-lipped, almond-eyed

Egyptian, her Midianite balm
seducing the courtyard,
the echo of her insistent psalm

of desire beating me like a hard
whip, and I ran from myself alone.

iii.
Dreams, always dreams. And change of raiment.
Not me, God read the seven fat and seven lean times right,
that I should be a signet on Pharaoh's pale wrist.

My new name pleased the soft-eyed daughter of the priest.
I loved this strange land from the Sea of Reeds to the back roads
 of Thebes.
In my sons were buried the afflictions of our race.

The barns were ready for the famished mobs.
Yes, praise Him, we did a good job.

iv.
They must be tested, with silver cup, with coin,
with rough speech, these betraying brothers
who sell their blood to coffle and barracoon.

They shake like sheaves withering
in the merciless drought of desert passage,
bound by shackling conscience tethering

them to unrelenting guilt, until His mercy
broke their bonds, my loud, pit-flooding tears.

v.
How does a father know a son come again,
prodigal, from entombing years
in a far city? Did he find in this Egyptian

prince under flying banners
wary eyes of my mother,
tentative smile at the corners

of lips of his dead lover?
And we wept long for her and each other."

MYTHOS

...what sacred games shall we invent...
— Nietzsche

I. The Temple

After Mystery, myth. And the archives of our stories:
Dogon arks and Pyramid texts
cavorting gods and shape-shifting tricksters,

plus Marvel's comic-book translations
with big-screen versions –
Beowulf to Ragnarok to Star Wars.

Mystery left to megachurches and mosques,
wayside shrines and Shaker yards,
vibrating crystals and palm readers.

But not in those counterfeit temples of distortion,
under the robes of pompous priests
or teleprompting of false prophets

will we find Mystery.
Into the catacombs of our death,
caverns of our defeat,

through the abyss of failure
enters the Light of the world
and Mystery tabernacles within us.

II. The Palace

Nimrod to Pharaoh to Babylonian moguls,
Alexander, Caesar, holocaust butchers of the Third Reich,
Asian megalomaniacs, southern caciques,

warlords from Genghis Khan to African tyrants
have plundered the holy places,
planted standards and busts before altars of incense,

recast their souls lost to Mystery
into mosaics of myth, legend and fable,
doomed to lava, forest, deep-sea coral —

palace intrigues, secret service assassinations,
Pendragon's tanks around the squares,
various Orwellian oppressions

guard their mythical power.
To our sacred barricades
humble weapons of faith,

anthems of love's covenants
come with fierce joy,
Our King's Mystery forever triumphant.

III.   The Town

For the hapless town, folktales and superstitions,
soap-operas, UFO sightings and bleeding statues,
days of the dead and Nostradamus

are the credible mysteries,
even as they negotiate petty dishonesties, taxes,
party-politics, crime, social-media scandals

hypocrisies and complacencies
compounded now by fake news.

Has irresponsible suffrage,
idolatrous political correctness,
damned unbelief

loosed ancient dragons and their beasts?
On a certain lane,
near a white cedar,

come visit if you like
the carpenter's shed
to face Mystery veiled in curling shavings, sawdust.

AFTER THE PSALMIST: SONG OF ASCENTS
A glosa variation

> *Now also when I am old and greyheaded,*
> *O God do not forsake me,*
> *Until I declare Your strength to this generation,*
> *Your power to everyone who is to come.* — *Psalm 71:18*

I draw near the high place —
bamboo-fluting of wood doves,
coconut palms shuttling the breeze,

Morne Gimie wreathed with overcast evening,
woodsmoke dissolving its plumes over Garrand,
anonymous traffic of voices, music, cars outside on the road

and news of another passing lingers
with intermittent drizzle
end-of-day gospelling blackbirds.

Now also when I am old and greyheaded,

still wanting that blood-warmth of affectionate arms
soft eyes of caring desire
lovingkind words that affirm,

certainties of covenant secure
against streetsmart chatter of infidelities
and mundane idolatries.

We finger insidious seductions of cyberspace
to distraction, shutting our hearts away
in virtual isolation with selfies.

O God do not forsake me

when names dodge familiar faces,
anxieties trouble sleep and speech, when
we collapse in once firm and potent places,

when dollars never meet estimated ends,
when newly-fashioned plantocrats
turn these hapless island-nations to big-boat destinations,

and the people jam streets with pagan noise
vote their birthrights to corrupt parliaments.

LORD, extend Your mercy to the young ones

Until I declare Your strength to this generation,

with my horn of words that sound true,
muted with love from blasted blaring
scaling the beauty of the blue

and other notes, measuring solo lines
with faith, bridging our earth
to Your great and Holy Kingdom.

Let us weave chords of canticles to birth
light again, counterpoint dark again,
to raise Your praise, to unveil again Your High Home,

Your power to everyone who is to come.

DOORS: AFTER CORRIE SCOTT, PHOTOGRAPHER

1. Entrances

First, cracked cement or tiled step-ups
come in off the road;
then, bruised storm-shutters (usually),
jalousies, cross-hatched lattices, glass louvres, curtains,
wondrous tin fretwork under rusted awnings,
thresholds launching varieties of door,
lintels, jambs and their firm frame of entry
rectangular portals
to particular lives.

2. Thresholds

to grandmothers and favourite cousins,
front-rooms, morris-chairs, crockery cupboards,
fading photos of ancestors gone to Panama,
last year's Sacred Heart almanac,
perhaps a Grundig radio and stereogram,
varnished table and varnished chairs
or woven straw-chairs and a plain-board covered table;
bedrooms behind other half-wedged doors,
certain smells and sounds of life (and sometimes dying);
through half-doors to kitchens,
enamel cups, clay goblet, old kettle
salt-fish roasting on a coalpot,
cobbled skin of breadfruits, chandeliers of ripening bananas,
match-boxes, bay leaves, a swizzle-stick,
full shelves and corners of all that loved paraphernalia.

3. Backways
Then you come to yards
with pomegranate and soursop trees,
heaps of stones with bleaching, blue-soaped clothes,

tall standpipe where you bathed, in naked glee,
noisy hens, pup watchful on its frayed cord,
and the clean latrine near the back fence,
a hibiscus hedge, its small leaning gate
cracking on the track to Bopère's two-room place,
partitions pasted with old newspapers...

4.   *Exits*
The pastel doors of the self-respecting poor
still face streets, roads, alleyways, corners
of bougainvillea lanes in old parts of town.
Ask Corrie Scott; she loves them.
In yards, dreadlocks bloodfire Babylon,
children stare into bleeping video-games
and babies splash in plastic tubs.
Beautiful doors close behind our hearts
as we step out in weave and tattoos,
name-brand shoes or slippers, tee-shirts and torn jeans,
or coat, tie and lap-top backpack,
ears charged with phone-buds,
to job, church, evening-classes or vendor hustle
to cremations or beach weddings, or divorce hearings
or whatever...

These hieroglyphs of old doors
these Rosetta Stones of once simple lives
are familiar palimpsests
that limn forever our first scrawlings of innocence
(remember those old school slates?),
our loud laughing under the mango tree
our hurt fists and angry heels
our devious seductions and brutal betrayals,
weepings, grievings, losings, floodings,
desperate faith-filled hopes to which we return
as to these doors and their certain welcome.

LOVE POEM : AFTER MOSERA

"Love?" she pouted, "Nah, not for me
I don't believe in it;
I living in the fast lane, dearie" –
lancing my foolish heart
with slit, searching eyes,

teasing me to heat
with her waiting, parting mouth,
several cleavages of tight
full body shifting about
the lucky couch.

Like the yellow-breast
battering a high window,
I'm caught at her address
under that vain flattering echo,
"She loves me, she loves me not…"

"ONE OF US HAS DIED"
In memoriam: Gandolph St. Clair (1951-2018)

One of us has died —
stilt-walkers, drummers and trumpeter on the big truck,
straggling mourners hiding

their distractions in embraces
of old friends
coming off sidewalks

to join the funereal shuffling
past harbour-front Government offices,

flag-draped City Hall, wooden Presbytery,
to file behind the varnished casket —
singular — its weight of grieving

on the aching palms of his abandoned
friends. In the Cathedral
self-serving eulogies go on

too long; he is beginning to fade
like the disintegrating holy frescoes

on which we gaze blankly. The plots of remembrance
thin, not thicken. Last conversations were about what?
Old quarrels were when? And what year did we go to France,

read in Toronto, smoke in Kingston?
Who thought he should have whatever or whenever?
Until a child's sobbing hits hard-fought

love, and we collapse beyond ourselves
behind the final leaflet-summary of our loss.

At the seaside cemetery,
his friend the priest sprinkles
holy rituals for the dead;

grave-men manoeuvre the box into the family tomb;
a scarved woman in shades carefully pours a palmful of petals;
his mother prays till every slab is laid; the drummers

chant Legba to open the gates, before the lone trumpet
sounds for the one of us who died.

HAIKU: AT 70

i.
On arthritic spurs
the aging cock'rel prances
to the chortling chicks.

ii.
The mango blossoms
above its shingled, brown bark,
stubborn, entrenched roots.

iii.
The dog peeps reluctantly
out its small window
at blustery rain.

iv.
Proprietary,
put out, the cat glares at us,
mewling plaintively.

v.
Well-lit, spacious rooms
books, memorabilia
unused plates, termites.

vi.
The green-hair dancer
stares past your idle glances
over fresh-laid wreaths.

vii.
The plunging sea-bird
bores the veined, heaving ocean
lifts the flying-fish.

MASQUERADE: FOR GARTH ST. OMER (1931-2018)

> *you wanted no career*
> *but this sheer light, this clear*
> *infinite, boring, paradisal sea...*
> *but never guessed you'd come*
> *to know there are homecomings without home.*
>   — *Derek Walcott*

Much has gone
like those wooden Bedford trucks
that took you down the coast,
like the demolished CDC apartments
and their ground-floor rumshops,
like burned-out Beaubrun House
top of Jeremie Street,
like the implacable power of the priests
their separating funeral bells
their reserved pews
their Latin masquerades.

Old parties of class
have transmogrified
to colour-coded camps
of political spite and petty vendettas;
more ole-mas', less costume,
more noise masking more desolation;
characters don't know
their own alienation
in this town posing as a city for tourist boats
taller than Morne Pavée.

Ah, but epiphanies surprise in Castries
near Broglie and Mary Ann
or was it Coral and St. Louis
when from down those gone, precocious years,

someone like our mothers calls our name
from her window-threshold under fret-carved fascias,
or from her mango and plum-tray corner,
open-faced, bright-eyes, gracious under her hat,
who blesses us with fruit and remembrances and a clear joy,
against all else, against all else.

PETROGLYPHS AND PICTOGRAPHS:
after Ron Savory (1933-2019) – In Memoriam

> ...*artefacts air-brushed from memory, teasing*
> *holograms in glass globules, daring translation:*
> *What can I make for you of those old bones, those scratched pebbles?*
> — *John Robert Lee*

i.   *earth: catacomb*

Earth-stones speak from Mazaruni galleries of petroglyphs
    and pictographs

murmur scratched names, carved mysteries, ancient runes
    of Rupunini
and lost El Dorado, hum through incised furrows

of weathers, planting seasons, favourite pets
engraved hieratic embraces,
excavate tablets of living faith

from shell-mounds and inundations –
                      our inheritance – these elemental artefacts
                                    sketches embedded
                                      in diurnal domesticities.

ii. *fire: ikon*

The scissor-tails carry fables of fire at their throats
cruising edges of oceans, half-believing
rumours of primordial Roraima,
falls from a distant Potaro,
a foolish boy with gulls' wings gone too near the sun.

The man who circles sea-birds with the palette of his gaze
sees them through canopies of abandoned forests

hears their clamour over surfing casuarina wind-breaks,
marvels they are not savannah vultures,
etches them coal-black ikons across the coral island of his love.

iii.   water: bark

His craft, he would tell you, was the simple bark of the spectral Arawak
navigating terrible silence under contentious macaws, toucans,
      squirrel monkeys,
boatman, alone on great Essequibo,
north-pointed past savannahs and forests,
psychedelic light pouring through soaring canopies
onto great vines, large leaves, pods,
the turning grace of herons in the swamps.

It carried him to the collage of Atlantic surf,
Caribbean vernacular, small-mountain ferns, sea-birds,
ancestral stones, familiar mythologies, the horned island of his rest.

iv.   air: heron

There's no migratory bird like the egret,
that cow-bird, world traveller

like Guyanese and other Caribbean children
colouring the diaspora.

Up the islands, through the airways,
down the Corentyne to Suriname,

across the border to Brazil,
New York, London, Dubai.

Now, we here, Ron, with you gone
further than all those territories of man's confusions,
probe neglected friendships, sketchy conversations, awkward love.

PART TWO

1. Desperate Notes

> *Take down the love letters from the bookshelf,*
> *the photographs, the desperate notes,...*
> — *Derek Walcott*

Sometimes, I'm naked in streets
or lost, anguished, in exitless ghettos,
or the road ends down a tangled ravine,

or, confused, I can't find my hotel
room or a place to pee – recurrent anxieties
troubled sleep –
                    Yeah, keep the not-so-subtle

psycho-babble, but why, you next to me, no more dancing
no more high tenor? Can't find you?

*

They say he wrote something
with blood from his slashed wrists
a final, absolute word

of realization, some profundity of the abyss
he was swallowing through his cold veins
his now-sober, emptying mind.

                              His best friend
recalls a sudden spurt of wind that whipped curtains round his
framed photograph which shattered like an unspeakable premonition.

I had bus fare, but chose to walk
through late Friday afternoon
fish-grills waking

beer-trucks delivering, inane
noise of sound-systems battering down Babylon
young girls half-naked
                              – didn't look at none –

but, like a crazy fool, watched your shut window for long
hours with the spy-glass of my filthy palms.

                              *

How come you didn't know me?
Your old dresses made the strips of rags,
busts came from your stained pillow,

your mother's madras covered your wigs,
you painted the shoes that self-same shade of yellow,
your torn panties covered my crotch.

                              Your bakanal heart make legs
in front my very eyes
and leave me a damn prancing fool.

When this clown reach Sheol
you will see who is who:
no masquerader and jester in hell,

no shabeen Delilah nor gap-tooth Jezebel anywhere,
no make-believe pardner
no ole-mas performer.

                        I standing like a stripper
down from the pole-vault of my bare, secret privates
in front the Man who know all my grief.

2. In the year that Shadow died

> *so don't tell me how love will rescue me,*
> *I was carnivorous about love, I ate love to the ankles,*
> *my thighs are gnawed with love*
> — Dionne Brand

> *...I knew instantly I had to go the hard way with you*
> *To learn how to love better.*
> *...We must go in the world: take taxis, trains,*
> *Responsibilities;...*
> — Hilary Davies

In the year that Shadow died and I turned 70,
and Gandolph St. Clair also died
and I saw England more truly

than before: South Bank, Cambridge, Notting Hill —
visited the Eltham sidewalk
where Stephen Lawrence was murdered;

Windrush was in the news again, aging immigrants deported;
I saw Kamara negotiate GPS and Uber
and knew that distant cities were for young bravehearts.

Watching late-night lovers strolling the Bankside,
sitting before Picasso at the Tate,
riding the bus to Peckham,

I wondered how, in the far
borough of aging libido, we could
find the way back to each other

with attention, affirmation and affection,
time-worn flirtations gone tender to touch,
smart-phone intrusions testing fidelity.

In the year that Shadow died, that griot from Tobago
wailing down the tracks
of his desperate notes

elemental and existential
excavating despairing desires
in the hungering, keening scales

he rode like a prancing Pierrot,
watching for something, something
in the naked eyes of revellers,

in the stripped eyes of lovers
in the tired eyes of old companions
in the mirror, in the mirror,

turning the years over
like an old-time vinyl LP
of Steel Pulse or Wailers

to try the other side of long-memoried pleasure,
affairs, brief liaisons, lost marriages.
It's always sex, the procreative,

the deep, lunging desire
for the impossible union
the perfect pairing,

for God, really. How else you explain
that perpetual empty space
out of which Shadow hopped

standing in the same place,
pulling from his guts
the plaintive chords of those lost

to themselves.
In the year I turned 70, body-weight
okay, reasonably good teeth,

some glaucoma, anxious libido
some mortgage to go, too few reviews
and fewer paid invitations to read

my poems of faith,
I wish, I wish I could say:
I saw God high and lifted up,

I understand my faith companion,
I trust my acquaintances,
I don't think of certain women,

I don't worry about my children's souls,
I trust the government,
I am not afraid of tsunamis

or being robbed
or being shot
or dying in a car wreck.

But then I think of that white woman cop
who shot Botham Jean in his Texas apartment
took him for a silhouette of a nigger

in his own apartment
eating cereal and watching American football.
She shot and killed Botham Jean, my son's school-mate,

and someone shot and killed
Kimberley deLeon
in her own house on Morne Fortune,

mother of two, a gentle beauty –
these cruise-ship destinations
are murder beach-fronts, bloody streets;

and I wish I could say
as I turn 70 in the same-size shoes,
the year Shadow died and Buju Banton came out of prison,

that everything go be okay,
that Queen Aretha's right about 'respect',
Aretha died the year Shadow died and Buju Banton came out of prison…

Hearing the rooster impatient for cool mornings
and the recurring canvassing of sunrise,
hawking away with hoarse crows,

watching overcast Plateau, Babonneau,
reggae down the road, children maddening the dog
with their running, I wish I could say all okay,

but not till Kingdom come
not till apocalypse
not till Jah show Himself,

for which roosters
are crowing hoarse,
distant Morne Gimie gone under haze.

3. Mystery sentences Himself to dance in solitary

> *I am the Alpha and the Omega, the Beginning and the End, the First
> and the Last.* — Jesus Christ (Revelation 22:13).

> *...I imagine you*
> *like these children, dancing*
> *in the deluge, naked as holiness.*
> — *Kwame Dawes*

Mystery sentences Himself to dance in solitary,
masked in the alphabet of flowering shrub, cock-crow, wood-dove,
lamb, jack-fish, morne, quarter-moon, constellation and nebulae,

simple Sovereign of the alleys, beaches, luminescent
evenings of galaxies, bouquet hedges of bougainvillea
candelabra of mango blossom.

                                        But if you wait and listen
you will hear His Man of sorrows crack His midnight robber word
in the prancing parade of the great Kanaval.

*

Is the same Man here
yesterday, today and everlasting tomorrow,
the veracity of my fortitudinous affection

hour upon every locust-devouring hour for you
is broadcast in the furthest regions of the reality
that fools cannot know.
                                  I Man here like your shadow
steadfast like a crucifix
my ear-lobe pin to your doorpost.

That the Ineffable should choose this shack,
costume of a poor fool,
bells and whistles of a pretentious joker,

sly faces of a cunning masquerader, foul
mouth of a cruel jester,
horned heart of a hurting clown:

                                Impossible
fantasy shout the mockers,
as they pelt the Holy Idiot with their cursings.

                                *

The whip of my sharp tongue
is not for you
the ugly of this long face

is for the wicked and worthless –
woe be unto them
high-class and low-class pretenders –

                              Not for you
vexation, only the searching eye of my compassion,
silent lips of my bare heart, my ungrateful love-child.

This Papa Djab jumbie digging in your garbage –
you cross the road, you curse, you rude,
you know the face, you know the name.

He beat his mother? He hate his father? He abuse
his sister? Or some woman eat his money
and make obeah with his manhood?

                        Maybe he come from heights
passing through the park, with an epiphany, to favour you,
you, afraid of discovery, you, hating to love?

                      *

It coming for these careless jokers,
these towns playing innercity,
batterers, bloodletters and child-killers,

these corrupt smilers and players
with people's lives, these fools
cover in their damned smartness,
                                no pity
from stick-lash of tsunami, exploding mountain of earthquake
blood fire, all that I seeing,
                      tired of crying over them.

You come under the casuarinas, near food-huts,
put your folded clothes under a beach-stone
not far from the tattooed girls, dancehall noise of smoking youths,

tourists topless on beach chairs, hotel security staring at you,
try to find a clear pool at the soughing edge
of the warm water.
                         In the all-embracing

massaging palms of sea-salt, you contemplate
the Mystery of that circling scissor-tailed sea-bird watching you.

4. And then came those caped crusaders

> *some people have hopes and dreams*
> *some people have ways and means"*
>   – Bob Marley

> *As though the colonials, the Tribe Traders*
> *and all the pharaonic masquerades of gone times*
> *were not fair threat.*
>   – Canisia Lubrin

And then came those caped crusaders, Marvel masqueraders,
Phantom and Zorro in my childhood newspapers and comic-books,
Batman and Lone Ranger in Saturday morning movie serials,
Spiderman, Captain Amerikkka and who else in 3D Cinemax,
white male machismo, supermen, saviours of dystopia
impossible mind-washing Hollywood
translating to jouvert picong come kanaval.

Now they battle cyborg villains
in the virtual reality of our video-game heads,
come-lately conquistadors, old imperial whitewashing
in high-speed pixels, digital delusions,
mythologies repackaged, gods and titans,
white witches, golden dragons and shape-shifters at it again.

But the good guys always win
which proves, if you will take it, some revelation
out of antiquity, out of the genesis of our history,
not just the race stuff, gender wars or recycling half-brother sagas,
but some seminal truth about why we are where we are
in this fantasia-arcade, this star-wars never-ending sequel,
perpetual coming of Superman and E.T.
hankering after Atlantis, Narnia and Wakanda –
the God and Man scenario
angelic civil wars in the avenues of the third heaven

strong rumours of a great King
strange prophecies of a strange, nailed Holocaust
and amazing confrontations in Hades.
Some swear to final defeat of the dark lord
and the death of death
of which Hollywood is a strange griot of our time.

Pierrot, that jester, old fool,
watching high-definition tv in the store-window
with a small crowd late Saturday
opines, like a clown, they could keep their Planet Krypton
their Valhalla, land of Oz, land of nothing-there,
jail-birds Lex Luthor and the Joker,
but he following his wayside-church godmother,
he taking Eden and all that coming through there:
flood, Babel, Sodom, Goliath, weeping Jeremiah
– he love the wheels in the wheels and the fire-chariots –
shepherds and three wise men round the feeding trough,
Golgotha, empty sepulchre, the Celestial City,
the loving, merciful Father
he never had.

5. Who made me a stranger in my world?

> *Life without music...*
> *Give me back my radio*
> *Some o' dem call him Uncle Sam*
> *Some o' dem call him Uncle Tom*
> *Uncle Sam and Uncle Tom*
> *Is dey are the same man*
> *Tief of music*
> *Steal away music...*
> — Steel Pulse

> *Let's start a conversation. Ask me where I'm from.*
> *Where is home, really home. Where my parents were born.*
> *What to do if I sound more like you than you do.*
> *Every word an exhalation, a driving out.*
> — Vahni Capildeo

> *My name is Bordeaux and Nantes and Liverpool and New York*
>   *and San Francisco*
> *not a corner of this world but carries my thumb-print*
> *and my heel-mark on the backs of skyscrapers and my dirt*
>   *in the glitter of jewels!*
> *Who can boast of more than I?*
> — Aimé Césaire

Who made me a stranger in my world?
Who determined I was a minority?
Who made my skin a boundary and barrier

to negotiate at immigration counters?
Who are the traffickers and traders
of bodies and souls and sex of the inheritors of the earth?

Who are the invaders of unfenced gardens
honest kitchens, sacred grounds?
who are the thieves of our acres, our wide rivers,

the surf-edged coasts of our children and old women?
Whose guns, burning crosses and mitred corruptions
lynched and raped and decimated nations and continents

of citizens – not minorities, not niggers, not coolies –
of this denuding blue-green planet angling around our sun?
Whose recurring post-truth narrative, recycling apartheid

red-neck latitudes of fenced plantations
and other such discriminations
we citizens – no resident aliens – reject and bloodfire?

Whose fingerprints are on every coup d'état,
regime-change manipulations,
behind caravans of refugees, over tent-cities,

on bleeding children in the streets of Herat,
rubble cities of Syria, atrocities in Sudan
charity scams and child abuse in Haiti?

And what of Trayvon, Charleston Church, the boy Tamir Rice,
    Sandra Bland,
Botham Jean in Texas, Jamal Kashoggi, all those neighbourhood
    assassinations?
You think I stretch the inventory too far, am mixing murders
    and metaphors,

don't know the histories
am disregarding tribal warfares, who sold who,
crusades, ancestral hatreds?

Costumes and masquerades evolve
but who are Babylon, Egypt and Rome today?
Who threatens and invades?

Who buys and sells house-slave leaders,
infiltrates democracies
interferes with elections?

Who spies and kills with drones
lies as a matter of policy,
hacks your private conversations?

Who arrogantly calls themselves super-powers,
whose lackeys insult you in the visa office,
whose police and soldiers shoot citizens with impunity?

David Hinds, roots-man of Steel Pulse, chanting them down
"snakes in the grass, they know not God,
politricksters…is dey are the same man".

My 92 year-old friend the songwriter
never forgot British headmaster Fox-Hawes
in the arena of a classroom

caning Bastien with 12 strokes
for burning the blackbook of detentions;
and Bastien never spoke.

Bravo Bastien, bravo citizen!
Bravo Rosa Parks, Mandela, Marley,
Toussaint L'Ouverture, Tiananmen Square tank-confronter,

Palestinian sling-shot warriors, Malala Yousafzai,
Liu Xiaobo, Mahatma Gandhi, Marcus Garvey
and all those who in the belly of the beasts

walk with disenfranchised coalitions,
raising blood-stained placards, berth-rights,
rainbow passports of citizenship,

claiming their place at the table,
their seat on the bus,
their desk in the school,

their home in the tree-lined avenue,
their voice in the senate,
their right to stroll in the park,

to wear their hair as they please,
without being raped,
without being shot in the back,

to check into any hotel,
to drive the car of their choice,
to love, to live.

6. Ars poetica

(for Esther Phillips, Poet Laureate)

Yet why not say what happened?
Pray for the grace of accuracy
Vermeer gave to the sun's illumination…
— Robert Lowell

…the metaphor is an aggressive attempt at clarity not secrecy. The poem addresses the reader, it asks the first question, it is not interested in the reader's comfort nor a narrative solution. It is not interested in your emotional expectations, or chronologies. It is flooded with the world. The great interrogation room is the stanza, you are standing at its door.

— Dionne Brand

You must now enter the silence alone and listen. Wait.
Wait for the translation of the first line. Write.
Write with your fingers searching the pigments on the palate
for the essential shading of the right
image. The medium frames the sacred intercession.

To give face, posture and voice to the holy is no trite
matter. And where humility unveils some gracious incarnation,
offer first this blessed sacrament to the King of saints.

*

Some would say all poetry is ekphrastic,
rising with intuition to theme, line, palette, pixel
of painting, carving, photograph, the art of life

responding with literal or oblique synonymous meaning –
how about erotic? The foreplay of lipping and tonguing
seductive verbs, hard nouns, some flattering adjectives,

erection of firm stanzas over flowing imagination
the coming together of the last line and exhausted conclusion.

*

Learn from Shadow, solitary,
mighty kaiso griot, how to put the story:
hear in your ear a prancing line,

chant extension of syllables through waving melodies,
phrase in the cave of your palate amazing phrases
straight from the yard behind the galvanise;

ricochet and dingolay down in the common life you come from,
stand up jumping in the parade of stanzas with your rough voice.

*

Not just the hard structure of logic, perfect architecture
of turning line, clever caesura, lurking tone of meaning;
not just extended, smart metaphor,

but how to bring the backward glance of the coupled heart
with the tender fervour of Creole violons, Malavoi harmonies
Patrick St. Eloi, konpa horns from Haiti,

because words must swing too, must flirt too
whatever the story, whatever the mood.

After all, after waiting, waiting for the first line,
for decorative words to clothe the skeletal idea,
for the shaping flow of meaningful imagination

married to the truth of the thing you see and hear,
hoping for the touch of sheltering beauty
and taste of harmony for which you almost despair –

when it does appear, you wonder with a hopeless prayer,
what's it for? with whom can I share?

*

Ex nihilo, out of nothing,
on to the void of the page of the screen
the narrative begins, again and again –

light in the urban darkness, recurring hope of heavens, reality of troubled earth,
planting thought to give seed and fruit, galaxies telescoped for alien signs,
seabirds and flying-fish for metaphor, beasts and creeping things for symbol –

and always, always, it's about naked Man and Woman
disputing for rest in the garden of their God.

7. The photos in obituary pages still surprise us

> *"What if this present were the world's last night?*
> *Mark in my heart, O soul, where thou dost dwell,*
> *— John Donne*

> *And even though it all went wrong*
> *I'll stand before the Lord of Song*
> *With nothing on my tongue*
> *But Hallelujah!*
>
> *— Leonard Cohen*

The photos in obituary pages still surprise us
that *so-and-so* has died, death has come to *her,*
we are still shocked by these chronicles,
as though this was some strange event
an alien invasion from space,
unfamiliar, incredible and unbelievable.

Pierrot, our masquerading friend,
in the sandy graveyard by the sea
at the funeral of his wayside-church godmother, Miss Bertha,
contemplates the hollow grave-mouth, the covering coffin,
her out-of-reach love, her creole bread and yellow butter, lime squash,
her painful passing: from his arms awkward around her shoulders,
her final sudden open eyes and smile upon him
before the rattling of the throat and last green bile.

So strange, all of it, he muses, sitting on a beach-stone,
watching seabirds dive for fish, waves eternally coming and going,
a couple in the water locked together, oblivious of tourists,
of the final hymns from the wreath-covered grave of Miss Bertha
so strange, so surprising, all of it.

Maybe Miss Bertha sent that brown heron to settle near him,
to look at him so intently, to tell him in his eyes

the Apostolic Mystery, that yes,
death is a Jab-Jab invader, a mako jumbie,
has to be, not after Miss Bertha's love for him.
How can that love die? How it can go in a hole in Choc cemetery?
And yes, death go die one day
when Resurrection morning come, when the Trumpet sound,
when Lord Christ come down
from that beautiful crystal evening-sky over Martinique
where the brown heron and the white seabird just gone.

Miss Bertha.

ABOUT THE AUTHOR

JOHN ROBERT LEE (b. Saint Lucia 1948) has published several collections of poetry. His short stories and poems have been widely anthologised. His books include *Saint Lucian* (1988), *Artefacts* (2000), *Canticles* (2007), *Elemental* (2008), *Sighting* (2013), *City Remembrances* (2016), *Song and Symphony* (2016), *Collected Poems* 1975-2015 (2017.) He compiled and edited *Roseau Valley and other poems* for Brother George Odlum (2003), *Bibliography of Saint Lucian Creative Writing 1948-2013* (2013); he co-edited *Saint Lucian Literature and Theatre: an anthology of reviews* (2006) with Kendel Hippolyte and co-edited *Sent Lisi: poems and art of Saint Lucia* (2014) with Kendel Hippolyte, Jane King and Vladimir Lucien. In 2017 he compiled and co-edited with Embert Charles *The Road to Mount Pleasant: Selected essays on Saint Lucian Culture in honour of Msgr. Patrick Anthony* on his 70th birthday. In 2019, Papillote Press issued his *Saint Lucian writers and writing: an author index*.

"Robert Lee has been a scrupulous poet, that's the biggest virtue that he has, and it's not a common virtue in poets, to be scrupulous and modest in the best sense, not to over-extend the range of the truth of his emotions, not to go for the grandiose. He is a Christian poet obviously. You don't get in the poetry anything that is, in a sense, preachy or self-advertising in terms of its morality. He is a fine poet."
 – Derek Walcott, Nobel Laureate 1992.

"One major Caribbean poet remarked that 'we all know that Robert's poems are often brilliant, remarkable and illuminating, and we know that we are faced here with one of our big poets who has built his career in relative silence.' But in silence, he has worked – "beyond talent/ beyond award,/ beyond tomorrow's tomorrow" – chronicled his times, from within the limits of geography, of having to live in a single body, in a particular time and circumstances, but with, as Walcott said of Chamoiseau, "an amplitude of heart". Even amid his certainty of the "promised parousia" and his visions of apocalypse, there is no shortage of tenderness, empathy, a complex humanity and indeed a love and feeling of privilege of having lived among remarkable and ordinary men, within his 'beautifully insignificant' island and city."

– Vladimir Lucien

ALSO BY JOHN ROBERT LEE

Collected Poems 1975-2015
ISBN 9781845233518; pp. 180; pub. 2017; £10.99

These poems tell both of a continuing journey and a subtly changing voice but also of an underlying, consistent attempt to hold together in one space the things that matter. This is seeking first the kingdom of God; maintaining the community of men and women who incarnate that kingdom and make life meaningful; the beauties of St Lucia's natural world and its rich traditions of folk-culture; and the challenges and demands of poetry.

Whilst sometimes Lee's poems involve a quiet self-communing, more often they are conversations with God and with those people who are close to him. At points they rise to being canticles of praise that express the experience of, or the yearning for the transcendent through the imagery of the visible world. And whilst the poems connect to the wider world of travel and world affairs, their touchstone is always St Lucia; they demonstrate how possible it is to find an enriching, puzzlingly complex and intellectually stimulating world in a small island society.

The journey the poems tell is from the young man enthused with the energy of the radical decolonizing spirit of the 1970s, the years of deepening of Christian faith to the present of maturity and the acceptance of loss as well as gain, and the stamina needed for the continuing struggle for St Lucia to emerge from its colonial past and be ever more itself. In the later poems there are more glimpses of the private man who recognises that "My heart holds rooms I've never entered/ doors concealed, secret entrances." And whilst over the forty years of the poems one hears always a personal, signal voice, over time the poems increasingly invest in the Kweyol language of the St Lucian folk as well as the voice of the English master and, latterly, display an growing interest in the relationship between poetry and the visual arts.

"... a testimony of the significance and high quality of contemporary St Lucian literature. His is a voice that has recorded its history, journeyed on its waves, refracted the lucent Caribbean light, its community and the kingdom of God – all with care, lyricism, heart and intelligence."

— Sudeep Sen